THE MEDIEVAL SURGERY

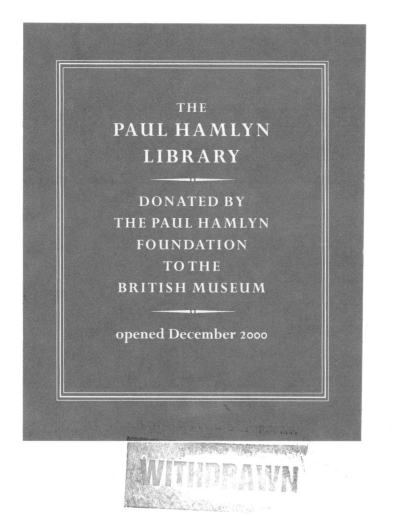

feiz auient que li chef nere de plaies
est plaie en plusurs ma ke auenent
neirs. Auchune feiz od la al chef.
clespesceur del test. Auchune
feiz sanz despesceur del test. od
la despesceur del test est quant
la plaie est achune fie grande
& a perte. Achune feiz petite. Meis quant la plaie pe
tite u grande. Lune est od graunde e large plaie. elau
tre est od petite estroite plaie. la despesceure del test qua
unt aueint ele od la blesceure des toies del ceruel est trut
dif atiendre. kar alchune feiz est blesce la toie que de
fent le ceruel est deltest que est apele la dure meire.
Auchune feiz la toie que est sur le ceruel que est apele la
pie meire. Si la dure meire est blesce ceo est la toie que de
fent le ceruel del test. par ces signes le deuez saner. la teste
del plaie li doit chuler. la face li doit roger. laueine des oiz
li deit treesuer. E la lange li doit tote neirtir. En apres qua
unt la pie meire est blesce ceo est la toie que est sur le ceruel
Par ces signes le deuez cunustre: li naffre recueta. E sa uoi

THE MEDIEVAL SURGERY

Tony Hunt

Fellow of St Peter's College, Oxford

THE BOYDELL PRESS

First published 1992 by The Boydell Press, Woodbridge
Reprinted 1994
Reprinted in paperback 1999

The Boydell Press is an imprint of Boydell & Brewer Ltd
PO Box 9, Woodbridge, Suffolk IP12 3DF, UK
and of Boydell & Brewer Inc.
PO Box 41026, Rochester, NY 14604–4126, USA
web site: http://www.boydell.co.uk

ISBN 0 85115 324 0 hardback
ISBN 0 85115 754 8 paperback

A catalogue record for this book is available
from the British Library

Library of Congress Catalog Card Number: 92–25411

This publication is printed on acid-free paper

Printed in Great Britain by
St Edmundsbury Press Ltd, Bury St Edmunds, Suffolk

Contents

*Figures in square brackets indicate the original Book and Chapter numbers to which the illustrations refer

For Kate

Acknowledgements

The fifty-one drawings from Trinity College, Cambridge, MS 0.1.20, which form the subject of this book, are reproduced by permission of the Master and Fellows, Trinity College, Cambridge.

I am extremely grateful to Peter Murray Jones, Librarian of King's College, Cambridge, for generously revising my descriptions and making many valuable suggestions.

Thanks are also due to Dr David McKitterick, Librarian of Trinity College, Cambridge, for facilitating the reproduction of the illustrations.

Introduction

What to call this little book? 'Medieval Surgery' or '*The* Medieval Surgery'? Hesitation is natural, because before the fourteenth century the boundaries of medicine and surgery were indistinct, not to say fluid. Until the eleventh century, surgery was not distinguished from the rest of medical practice at all. During the course of the twelfth century, the achievements of Arabic medicine (itself of course indebted to Greek medicine, especially the Hippocratic corpus) were made available through Latin translations and a body of specialized knowledge was thereby consolidated. This led to a greater interest in the specific possibilities of surgical practice. Surgery remained, however, a much broader field of activity than is suggested by the modern use of the term. In Italy, where the treatise illustrated in these pages was produced, there are few signs of any clear separation of medicine and surgery even as late as the thirteenth century.

Of course, 'cutting' was by no means the sole, or even principal, activity of surgical practitioners who, besides incision, frequently had recourse to physical manipulation (in the setting of fractures and dislocations), to the external application of a wide variety of medication in the relief of bleeding, infection and pain, and to the cleansing and dressing of wounds. Thus, while some external injuries (e.g. cranial fractures, ulceration, fistulas) undoubtedly called for incision/excision (and thereafter suturing) or cauterization, and certain internal injuries necessitated venesection and cupping, surface lesions such as tumours and swellings might simply invite the application of ointments (surgical treatises contain numerous receipts for the preparation of medicaments of many kinds). The treatment of eye complaints, on the other hand, particularly the use of the needle to remove cataracts (couching), seems often to have been a speciality. On the whole the scope of surgical intervention was limited, the variety of techniques restricted, and the number of instruments and appliances at the disposal of the surgeon modest. All this encouraged caution and also attention to alternative therapies. Professional rivalries (including the barber-surgeons), demarcation disputes, controversies concerning the treatment of wounds all came later than the treatise considered here.

It is clear from the illustrations accompanying this treatise that the *medicus* is depicted practising both surgical intervention in the strict sense (fig. 1, trepanation) and the external application of medicaments such as ointments (fig. 15). Both types of treatment take place in a dispensary in which are kept surgical instruments (fig. 2) and *materia medica* (fig. 3) and which is the scene of the making up of medicines as well as the treatment of patients. To employ a modern term (first used in this sense last century), it is a surgery. Hence the title finally judged most appropriate for this book.

The text which is the subject of the illustrations in this book is a significant one in the history of surgical writing in Europe. With the fall of Alexandria in 643 AD the medieval West effectively lost touch with writing on surgery for almost five centuries. The *Compendium of medicine* or *Epitome* by Paul of Aegina (AD 625–690) contained 122 chapters (= Book 6) on surgical therapy and a large section (Book 4) devoted to the general treatment of wounds, but whilst it continued to be influential in the evolution of the rapidly developing Arabic medicine, it remained almost unknown in the West where the striking advances of Arabic medicine seem to have played little part in the revival of surgical writing. When the revival came it took place in northern Italy in the course of the twelfth century. The prime mover in this revival seems to have been a rather obscure figure, Roger Frugard, who lectured in Parma and is now thought to have no connection with Salerno despite historians' continuing practice of referring to him as Roger of Salerno. Roger of Parma, as we may justifiably call him, was not himself an author, but in the 1170s Guido of Arezzo the Younger and a team of Roger's pupils set themselves to the task of assembling and editing lecture notes on Roger's teaching and in c.1180 issued the product of their labours as the *Chirurgia* ('Surgery'). Over twenty manuscripts of this important Latin treatise survive, the earliest being from soon after 1200. From an examination of its contents there emerges a picture of Roger as a teacher of independent and pragmatic stamp, who was able to correct the deficiencies of his predecessors through his own intelligence and operative skill. He cites few authorities and himself had little influence on subsequent writers of surgery, though his work maintained its authority for several centuries. For at least a century and a half it was not only copied and translated, but also conflated with commentaries and supplementary notes to form a tradition of intimidating complexity. Paradoxically, the first stage in this arduous process of glossing and amplification took place c.1200 in Salerno, the centre where historians had long located Roger's own activities as a teacher.

The first translation of the *Chirurgia* into a vernacular language was made in southern France and was really an adaptation into verse of Books 1–3, apparently the work of Raimon of Avignon who completed it by 1209. It then looks as if Roger's treatise was translated into French prose in the first half of the thirteenth century and also into Anglo-Norman prose in England in the same period. The evidence for this is provided by MS O.1.20 in the library of Trinity College, Cambridge. This is a large and extremely important collection of vernacular medical texts, mostly of continental origin but copied in England by a variety of insular scribes. The drawings it contains are the subject of this book.

On ff. 24va–30rb of the Trinity manuscript there survives part of a translation which, in the light of some of its vocabulary, we should probably assign to the north-east of France, but which was certainly copied in England. It covers no more than Books I,1–3, 5–8, 11–22, 25–6 and III,27. The first book of Roger's treatise deals with headwounds and at the bottom of f. 24va there is a drawing of a man with a long club striking the head of another man who is holding a spiked mace.

This isolated illustration is certainly the work of the artist who provided the drawings for the complete Anglo-Norman translation

of Roger's treatise which is found later in the manuscript: one has only to observe the characteristic wrinkles in the lower sleeves of the figures' garments, the dynamic leg movements of the assailant, the typical headgear of the figure with the mace, the characteristic avoidance of profile in the depiction of the face, and the representation of blood in the rubricator's red ink, exactly as on f. 240r (fig. 2). It therefore looks as if an artist was commissioned to illustrate the vernacular translation of Roger's treatise and that, coming to the text on ff. 24va–30rb, he produced a single drawing before realising that this was only a fragment and that the complete translation was to be found on ff. 240r–299v.

For this second text the artist provided forty-eight line drawings, some of which are tinted in yellow, brown and green (the opening initial, fig.1, is not by him and was executed at the same moment as the text itself; the isolated, incomplete drawing, fig. 50, is also by another hand). This translation was certainly produced in England, for the writer has included a number of indigenous names ('en englés'): henbane, maddok, cockle and the hybrid 'popi noir'. The artist finished drawings to accompany Book I (on headwounds) and Book 2 (diseases of the neck and throat) as far as chapter 15, thus covering about half the text of the treatise. Despite this limitation his work is outstanding on a number of counts. The refined technique of the drawings will be evident from the reproductions in the following pages, particularly in the carefully arranged multiple folds of the draperies which produce a marvellously plastic effect. Then there is the artist's highly developed decorative sense, his delight in variety of design, which finds expression in the inexhaustible inventiveness with which he treats certain recurring features such as the doctor's chair and the range of medical jars and vessels in the dispensary (he is largely indifferent to footwear, though there is some decoration in figs. 3, 4, 13, 36 and he depicts clothes-fastenings in figs. 4, 7, 10, 34, 35). No less striking is his acute sense of psychology which through the eloquence of facial expressions and gestures imparts a sympathetic humanity to medical scenes which elsewhere can often seem brutal, callous or indifferent. Equally satisfying is the artistic disposition of each scene, in which a concern for balance and symmetry is a prominent feature. The artist's exceptional skill in harmonising technical, aesthetic and emotive considerations make him a unique figure in the story of thirteenth-century British manuscript illustration. But who was he and when did he work?

His personal identity inevitably eludes us, but it seems certain that he had received specialist training in medical illustration and had sufficient linguistic skills to ensure an accurate understanding of the Anglo-Norman text. For the most part his illustrations follow the text closely, though the last few drawings (figs. 46, 47, 49, see also fig. 18) unaccountably bear only a loose connection with the sections of text they accompany. The artist's very individuality, however, increases the difficulty of dating his work, for nothing comparable has survived in insular manuscripts. There has been a tendency to place his activity in the period c.1230–40, or even earlier, but here we need to be cautious. It is clear that the drawings were executed after the text was copied – no space was left for them and they all appear in the bottom margin of the page (which was, lamentably, cropped in the eighteenth century). It is difficult to date the two scribes responsible for copying the Anglo-Norman translation of the *Chirurgia*, but their work could easily be as late as 1250. There are no firm grounds, therefore, for situating the artist's activity in an earlier period.

Even less certain, of course, is the length of time over which the artist was working. We can see that he illustrated less than half the text. There are signs of incompleteness in several of the drawings. For example the patient's seat is not executed/completed in figs. 18, 19, 32 and the assistant's seat is missing in fig. 44. A few drawings are conspicuously less successful than the rest and this may be due to haste: fig. 40 displays strangely poor proportions and posture in the patient; in fig. 45 there is an unnatural stiffness in the patient's leg position: the assistant's posture in fig. 47 is ambiguous. These flaws occur towards the end of the series. On the other hand, quite early on there are signs of a rather one-dimensional approach to the placing of the patient's hands, especially when he is leaning forward: they are not clearly anchored in fig. 14 and in fig. 19 the patient's hands seem to miss the doctor's knees and upper legs completely (compare fig. 5), a similar effect being in evidence in fig. 41. By and large, though, the artist works meticulously. It is interesting to see how a displacement of materials in his text (due to faulty copying) i.e. I,45–II,3 (figs. 20–22), causing II,2 to be split in to two separate sections, led him to illustrate the sewing of the neck-wound twice (figs. 22 & 41). The small signs of haste and lack of completion coupled with the fact that the artist got only halfway through the text may suggest that he was interrupted, perhaps by death. In the latter eventuality it is possible that fig. 50 is a pious tribute to him by a colleague.

However this may be, we should be grateful that the artist executed the drawings with such love and devotion. Not only do they provide a precious insight into medieval medical practices and a rare sense of aesthetic satisfaction, they also serve as useful guides, in addition to the red rubrics of the text, to the contents of the various chapters of the *Chirurgia*, thus providing instantly recognizable markers which facilitate the practical consultation of the treatise. The illustrations must have been reassuring to doctor and patient alike, and today they can give pleasure to even the most casual reader.

Reference

See N.G. Siraisi, *Medieval and Early Renaissance Medicine: An Introduction to Knowledge and Practice* (Chicago / London, 1990) ch.6; M.-C. Pouchelle, *The Body and Surgery in the Middle Ages*, tr. by Rosemary Morris (Cambridge, 1990); O.H. & S.D. Wangensteen, *The Rise of Surgery: From Empiric Craft to Scientific Discipline* (Minneapolis/Folkestone, 1978).

Note on the illustrations

The illustrations are reproduced same size, with the exception of p.4, which appears same size on the frontispiece.

The Medieval Surgery

1. *Consultation for Headwound* [I,1; f.240r]

The text of Roger's *Surgery* begins with an illuminated initial A which was executed by a different artist from the one responsible for the more refined line drawings in the rest of the text. Against a brownish-red ground the illustrator has depicted the *medicus* cross-legged in a pose of authoritative consultation, his assistant or *famulus* behind and to his left holding aloft a urinal (urine vessel) – uroscopy, or inspection of the urine, was a favourite diagnostic device – whilst the patient kneels before the doctor. The latter is dressed in a long surcoat and stalked round cap typical of the thirteenth century. The patient's head is bound with a strip and the doctor is making his diagnosis. A sense of close contact between consultant and patient characterises all the illustrations. The accompanying text deals with cranial fractures and headwounds which may involve damage to the meninges (or cerebral membranes), the *dura mater* and the *pia mater*. The facial expressions of the three figures are less interesting than those produced by the artist of the line drawings and there is a static impression which may suggest the doctor's thoughtful deliberation before arriving at his diagnosis. In the leg movements of doctor and patient, however, we find the same harmonious balance that is evident in the drawings. The clothes of all three figures are washed in green and the same colour has been applied to the urine vessel. The doctor's seat bears red decoration and some of the folds of the garments are also picked out in red. The saw-tooth decoration is in red and blue and there is simple red penwork ornamentation at the head of the initial.

2. Damage to the Cerebral Membrane and View of Dispensary [I,1; f.240r]

Within a double arcade, the arch and capitals of which are washed in pale yellow, the outer pillars in green, appear two distinct illustrations which represent a programmatic statement by the artist about his method of rendering the text. On the one hand, there are scenes depicting the diagnosis or treatment of ailments specified in the accompanying treatise; on the other, there are views of the dispensary which are almost always provoked by the appearance in the text of a lengthy receipt, or prescription, for a particular medicament. The artist thus here accurately reflects the dual nature of the text's contents, diagnostic and remedial, which covers surgical intervention of a technical kind complemented by more traditional therapeutic applications ranging from the simples of popular medicine to the compounds of a more sophisticated pharmacognosy. The first scene of this diptych depicts a consultation in which the patient's shaven head reveals a clearly visible wound which may have led to damage of one of the cerebral membranes. The doctor is shown in stalked, roll-brimmed round cap and has removed his right-hand glove so that he may direct the patient's responses. To his gesture of authoritative inquiry and instruction the patient responds with a movement of his right hand indicating compliance (perhaps also that he has been explaining his symptoms) whilst his left arm is held in a sling – he has presumably sustained his injuries on the battlefield. One of the symptoms of damage to the *dura mater* clearly advertised in the accompanying text is blackening of the tongue, here curiously

indicated (like the headwound) in red, and the doctor has thus asked the patient to stick out his tongue for inspection. The patient looks up into the air, whilst the doctor's eyes are clearly trained on the patient's tongue. The illustration shows the artist's careful attention to posture and exhibits an artistic symmetry, the doctor's raised right hand being balanced by that of the patient, whilst the latter's left hand in the sling forms a parallel with the doctor's left hand clasping the glove. Characteristically, there is scrupulous attention to facial expression, the drapes of the costumes, and the decorative detail of the seating – the patient's seat is apparently covered by the outer garment(s) of which he has divested himself. The doctor's glove and seat and the patient's sling are washed in yellow.

The depiction of the dispensary is particularly comprehensive. In the background are rows of storage jars of various shapes with lettering to indicate their contents. Many preparations were named by prefixing to their principal ingredient the Greek preposition *dia-*, which when used with the genitive plural had the sense of 'made from'. So on the top shelf we have DIAD = diadragant, made with gum tragacanth; DIAC[I?] = diaciminum, made with cumin; DIAP = diaprunis, made with plums; then APOS indicates Apostolicon ('ointment of the Apostles') and POP = populeon, made with poplar buds. On the lower shelf the letters read . . .IA; POST; DIA; DIA.

A receipt for the preparation of Apostolicon is in fact found on the verso of the following page. A much less conventional feature of the pharmacy is the set of surgical instruments which hang rather ominously from the lower shelf on the left-hand side of the illustration (see also fig. 44). They exemplify the artist's constant delight in variety of design and include mallet, borer, claw-bar and trepan. The dispensary seems to be carefully supervised by the doctor himself. He is shown with two assistants who do not always both appear in subsequent views of the dispensary. The scene is here artistically arranged with a set of balances hanging between the two assistants. The figure on the left is shown pounding drugs in a mortar – the use of two pestles is a consistent feature of this artist's dispensary pictures – while the one on the right stirs materials in a basin over a fire. The disposition of the whole scene is beautifully balanced, the drawing refined, and the technical details authentic. The ground between the storage jars is coloured green, as are the balances, mortar and spatula. A very pale yellow wash has been applied to the legs of the assistants.

3. *The Dispensary* [I,3: f.241v]

The second view of the dispensary, within an ochre-coloured frame, is inspired by the inclusion in the text of a receipt for the surgical preparation or ointment known as Apostolicon ('ointment of the Apostles'): *apostolicon cirurgicum* in the original Latin, *entrait cirugien* in the Anglo-Norman. The ointment is to be applied after the suturing of the headwound and involves melting naval pitch and wax over a fire, weighing out specific measures of ingredients (quantities are by no means always indicated in the prescriptions), pulverizing and placing in various vessels, here represented by four pouches arranged in a shallow dish. The supervisory role of the doctor is here given prominence by integrating him, complete with balances and tray of *materia medica*, in the picture. He is quite recognizably the same figure as in the preceding illustration, with an almost identical facial expression as he observes the work of his assistants as intently as he had done his patient. The artist's outstanding talent for lending a palpable quality to the drapes of the clothes is evident in all three figures, as is his meticulous attention to detail, which is shown in the variety of plants and medicaments on the tray and the inexhaustible inventiveness of his depictions of the physician's chair in which he scarcely ever repeats himself. The artist is a man to whom decoration is a source of pleasure which is never undervalued, whatever the technical demands of his subject. The absence of lettering on the storage jars (which are never depicted in the standard *albarello* design!) is probably an oversight, since their uniformity of design is likely the result of the need to provide space for such lettering (cf. fig. 8). The two colours used in this illustration are ochre and green, the latter appearing on the mortar, cauldron, some of the herbs on the tray, and on two of the pouches in the dish.

7

4. *Gauging the Size of a Headwound* [I,5; f.242r]

The illustration accompanies a section of text setting out directions for estimating the size of a headwound. These are that when penetration is deep and the wound narrow, the only way to assess the extent of the wound is by digital palpation, i.e. insertion of the finger into the opening of the wound. Thus the doctor, here depicted with hood (*aumuce*) raised, steadies the patient with his left hand and places the forefinger of his right hand in to the wound to explore, and if necessary, to enlarge it. The picture is closely related to the text, a fact which M.R. James failed to appreciate when he described the scene as a doctor smearing ointment on the head of a kneeling patient. The latter, who is always the natural focus of attention, supports himself on his forearms, his eyes averted. His posture beautifully effects the transition between the doctor and the bystander in barbette and fillet (or is it a crown? Sudhoff described her as a queen in crown and ermine). Her pose is of understandable anxiety and might suggest that she is the patient's wife; if so, certainly an aristocratic one. Like a modern dentist's chair – before it began to resemble a psychiatrist's couch – the doctor's seat provides the necessary height from which he can properly examine the headwound and at the same time balance the figure of the bystander. As often in the work of this artist, we have the perfect fusion of aesthetic, expressive and technical functions. The chair is coloured green and ochre, the edge of the lady's robe beyond the ermine also being green.

5. Examining and Cleansing a Headwound
[I,5; f.242v]

The double illustration is closely keyed to the accompanying text. The doctor, clearly recognizable again with his hood down, is using a razor to make a cruciform incision so that the flaps of skin may then be lifted or pulled back from the cranium in order to permit examination of the nature and condition of the wound. The assistant concentrates on holding the patient's head still. Surprisingly, the patient's head has not been shaved. The next stage of the investigation, after digital palpation and incision, is that, if not obstructed by haemorrhage, and assuming that a fragment of bone remains to be removed, the doctor should take a pair of surgical forceps ('teneilles', cf. fig. 10) to deal with it. This operation is duly illustrated in the right-hand picture which is conceived along the lines of a mirror image displaying the artist's constant concern for balance and equilibrium. It is almost as if the doctor is gazing at his mirror image rather than at the patient, who is also depicted in postures which complement each other in the two illustrations. There remains the figure in the middle. M.R. James thought that he was producing money from a bag, but it seems more likely that he is proffering *magdalions* which are mentioned in the preceding receipt for 'ointment of the Apostles' [I,4] and explained as 'une ronde confection' or cylindrical medicament which spicers call 'macdalions' and which are used for

10

anointing bone and placing on the wound after suturing. This double illustration includes two surgical instruments and raises the interesting question of technical terminology in the original Latin and the vernacular translation. In Latin, names of surgical instruments were quite well established and some MSS of Roger's *Chirurgia* include illustrations of the different instruments along with their names. In the vernacular, however, there was as yet no such tradition. The Anglo-Norman translator of Roger's treatise usually avoids the difficulty by reproducing the Latin, whether he understands it or not. The forceps are often known as *pi(ci)cariolus*, though there are many corrupt variants. The translator can render this by the familiar 'teneilles' and similarly the *rasorium* effortlessly becomes 'rasur'. But another instrument mentioned at this point in Roger's Latin text is a type of scraper called a *rugen* (or *rugina*) and here the translator does no better than write 'auchun ostil cirugien' ('a certain surgical instrument') which the artist is at a loss to render and consequently omits from the illustration. No colour is employed in this double scene other than splashes of yellow on the seats, the handle of the razor, and the pouch.

6. *Test for Cranial Fracture*   [I,6; f.243r]

The doctor is shown giving instructions to the patient from a book open on a reading stand, an obvious bit of propaganda by the artist for the sort of medical treatise which he is himself illustrating. The doctor is clearly depicted reading, his left hand raised in a gesture which indicates that he is issuing directions to the patient, who is complying. The test is to determine, in a situation where there is no obvious depression or swelling, whether fracture of the cranium has taken place or not. To this end the patient is instructed to stop up his mouth, nose and ears and blow hard. The escape of air or other matter would be a sign of a fissured bone and hence of cranial fracture. In scenes where he is passive the patient is normally shown seated, but the physical effort required of him in this instance has led the artist to portray him standing with his legs apart. M.R. James saw 'an excited patient with swelled face and hands on head', whilst Sudhoff thought that the patient was simply being informed that surgical intervention was necessary for his head injury and was reacting with understandable dismay. As usual, the artist has remained faithful to the contents of the accompanying text. For the first time, however, there is a change to the doctor's garment – it is lighter, with consequently fewer folds, no long sleeves and there is no hood. It is remarkable how the artist has lent movement to the doctor's right, and the patient's left, leg which conveys the sense of collusion or cooperation between the two. For the colouring there are simply modest touches of yellow on the lectern and the doctor's seat.

7. Cranial Fissure [I,7; f.243v]

This double illustration continues the instructions for dealing with cranial fissure and depicts two more surgical instruments specified in the accompanying text. The instrument used in the left-hand picture is a drill or borer which the Latin original calls *trepanum* – a sort of auger or trephine. The translation has 'un ostil que est fest cum un perçur que est apelé *trepacium*' ('an instrument shaped like a borer which is called a trepacium') – *trepacium* is a palaeographical error for *trepanum*. In the treatment of cranial fissure the scalp wound is enlarged and the cranium carefully perforated with a trephine at each side of the fissure so that the wound may be widened for the removal of discharges and bits of bone. This is done by connecting the holes bored on either side of the fissure with another instrument, a surgical chisel known as *spatumen*. This is illustrated on the right together with a mallet. The Latin of Roger's treatise has the name in the instrumental ablative *spatumine*. This defeats the translator who writes 'un cisol cirugien que est a cel oes fait que est apelé *spatumini*' ('a surgical chisel designed for this purpose called a spatumini'). These technical terms confer some degree of sophistication on a scene which M.R. James brutally described with the words 'doctor seems to be driving a crowbar into the man's head'. The postures of the patient are here new and expressive. On the left the patient, clean shaven, is half supine, his hand over his eyes, head held steady by the assistant as the obviously alarming task of drilling proceeds. On the right he is shown bearded, hands gripping knees in self-steadying posture, his head held between the knees of the doctor. In both illustrations the patient averts his eyes, whilst the doctor looks intently at the wound on which he is operating. The appearance of the surgical mallet, which is *not* mentioned in the text, demonstrates the artist's natural and practical understanding of the operation being described. The fastenings on the doctor's garments (see fig. 10) are yet another example of the artist's delight in varied decoration. Touches of green have been applied sparingly to the seats, the tip of the trephine and the head of the mallet.

8. *The Dispensary* [I,8; f.244r]

Another illustration of the dispensary, this time occasioned by a receipt for an embrocation ('embroke') or plaster, which in winter should be placed over the dressed wound until it begins to suppurate. The receipt includes as ingredients mallow, bear's-breech, dock, linseed, fennel etc. which are to be stirred over a low heat with a spatula – as in the illustration. The doctor seems to be represented by a 'locum' who is beardless and younger-looking and here holds a stirrer (cf. figs. 33 & 48). On the third shelf, below rows of unlettered vessels, there is a set of variously shaped jars including a horn and what looks remarkably like a Scottish stone hot-water bottle. There are flat dishes beneath, all testifying to the artist's highly developed decorative sense. His inventive chair designs continue to enrich the illustrations and the folds of the doctor's robe are treated with a consistent skill and attention. The assistant stirs the contents of the basin with a spatula, whilst holding in his left hand what is presumably a poker in order to regulate the combustion so as to maintain a low heat. The darker-coloured jars are green, which also appears on the seat and on the assistant's spatula. Splashes of yellow have also been applied to the seat and spatula and parts of the cauldron and jars.

9. A Home Visit [I,12; f.245v]

The illustration depicts the doctor, with a floriated staff reminiscent of the caduceus, attending the bed-ridden patient (again with shaven head) to determine whether or not he has sustained a fracture of the cranium. The doctor seems to be giving instructions to the patient, probably as part of an enquiry about his symptoms. The picture accompanies a section of text dealing with diagnosis from indications exhibited by the patient himself, up to the fifth or seventh day, concerning appetite, sleep, bowel movements etc. If the patient's performance of such functions is poor, cranial fracture is indicated. The patient's head is shaven and supported by a pillow as he sits up in bed. For the first time there is clear evidence of eye contact between doctor and patient. The artist positively relished the prospect of bedclothes and treated the full folds with his customary richness and depth. There are touches of yellow on the folds of the clothes, on the unhatched areas, on the seat and on the floriated head of the staff.

10. *Cranial Injury* [I,14; f.246r]

The accompanying text deals with the injury caused by a blow from a sword or by a stone or similar. The skin which hangs loose should be cut away with a surgical instrument called a *rugen* – a sort of scraper (cf. no. 5 above) – and loose bone thrown away. In fact the scraper is not illustrated here and this is probably because the Anglo-Norman translator botched the identification by writing 'un ostil cirugien que est apelé *rubigo*' ('a surgical instrument called a rubigo') which the artist not unnaturally found incomprehensible (*rubigo* means rust or blight), thus substituting another part of the operation, removal of a fragment of bone. This seems to offer a clear indication that the artist was following the Anglo-Norman text and not the Latin original. The doctor is shown holding a piece of bone in his left hand, whilst he holds a pair of forceps in his right hand – an entirely appropriate addition by the artist (cf. fig. 5). The doctor's robe is decorated with fastenings which appeared in an earlier illustration (fig. 7). There seems to be similar fastenings on his sleeves. This is one of the few illustrations which depart a little from the text, but not so radically as M.R. James thought when he described the scene as 'Doctor uses forceps and plug to head of kneeling man'. The patient seems much reduced in size. There are discreet touches of yellow.

11. A *View of the Dispensary* [I,15; f.246v]

This illustration accompanies the receipt for 'pudre ruge' (*pulvis rubeus*), a red powder placed on wounds to hasten the healing process. It is recommended for staunching blood, promoting the knitting together of bones and the generation of new skin. As in fig. 3, the doctor is shown as an active participant in the dispensing of prescriptions, the balances and tray of *materia medica* being once more in evidence. The hanging pouches resemble those already illustrated in fig. 3. The shields on the wall may simply reflect the artist's concern for symmetry and pleasure in decoration (cf. fig. 16). The drawing is apparently incomplete, but the artist's careful attention to details of folds and drapes is still evident.

12. *Nasal Injuries* [I,19; f.247v]

The doctor appears once more hooded (see fig. 4), but beardless. For the first time, since we are no longer dealing with headwounds, the patient is wearing a cap, which resembles that of one of the assistants in fig. 4. M.R. James described the scene as 'Doctor with fingers in mouth of patient', but in fact the accompanying text deals with injuries to the nose and in particular transverse cuts. Treatment involves placing a linen pad ('plumaceol') in each nostril to keep the position of the nose firm (a sort of nose-stall, 'apoial', *sustentaculum*, is also recommended). The operation is effected by touch rather than by sight and so the doctor stares into space. For the first time the patient is seated and so to compensate for the lack of leg movement the artist has depicted the doctor with legs crossed at an acute angle.

13. *Removal of Arrow from Headwound* [I,20; f.248r]

The patient's head is shaven so that the doctor can obtain a good view of the points of entry and exit. According to the accompanying text the patient is to be asked for details of his position when struck, so that further information about the arrow's likely trajectory may assist the doctor in his estimate of the wound. The arrow is to be moved gently to loosen it. The problem with this illustration is to identify the operation being performed by the doctor's right hand. It does not look as if he holds the arrow tip because the end is not pointed – if anything it is slightly splayed, so he may be holding a tent or pledget. Possibly the artist has anticipated a detail in the next chapter and depicted the doctor enlarging the exit wound with a trephine, in order to remove the arrowhead through this opening and then to withdraw the shaft of the arrow through the entrance wound. If the doctor *is* here enlarging the exit wound with some sort of small borer, then the state of the next section of text (I,21), concerning arrow wounds to the cranium, provides a possible explanation. In that section the Anglo-Norman translator has failed to recognize the surgical instrument *rugin(e)* (cf. nos. 5 & 10 above) and the scribe has simply left a gap in the manuscript. The artist was thus unsure what sort of instrument to depict, though he understood that the doctor's action was that of enlarging the wound. The patient's costume here includes a hood. There are very faint touches of yellow on the seat and the folds of the garments.

14. *Removal of Barbed Arrow* [I,21; f.248v]

This illustration depicts the removal of a barbed arrow, the patient being, for the first time, stripped to the waist. Book One of Roger's *Chirurgia* deals with headwounds, but the artist appears to have taken chapter 21 as being of more general application, hence depicting here a wound to the trunk. The instructions in the text are that the barbs of the arrowhead should be taken in a pair of forceps ('tenailles') and carefully pressed so that they are bent flush with the shaft, thereby facilitating withdrawal. Alternatively, a brass cannula or a number of goose-quills may be placed on each barb for the same purpose. The patient's breeches are a new feature of his dress (cf. fig. 43). M.R. James described him as having 'a markedly anxious expression'. The delicacy of the operation – what is depicted here is the neutralizing of the barbs, not the extraction of the arrow – rather than any sense of strain or effort is conveyed by the position of the doctor's legs in parallel with the patient's. The hatched area of the doctor's seat is coloured green, as are the forceps: for the first time green is used on the folds of the garment. There are faint splashes of yellow on the seat and on the folds of the patient's garment.

15. *Treatment for Tinea* [I,23; f.249v]

According to the text, one type of tinea is incurable and no sufferer should be accepted for treatment, but there are two other varieties which are susceptible of cure. The first stage is the shaving of the patient's head as depicted in the illustration. The doctor is here shown looking at the assistant to whom he is giving instructions symbolized by his manual gestures. These concern the administration of an ointment for up to nine or eleven days, or such time as the doctor determines, for which Roger's treatise supplies a receipt. There is a second receipt, for a depilatory cream ('psilotrum'). The assistant is thus shown holding a jar of ointment, anointing the patient's head, and seated, since he himself is applying the remedy. The patient, who looks comfortable, sits on the ground to facilitate administration of the ointment. Here he is at his most passive, gazing vacantly into space. This is one of a number of scenes where the doctor is shown treating the patient apparently in the dispensary itself. The storage jars are coloured alternately yellow and green. There is, unusually, a splash of blue on the right-hand end of the shelf and on the scroll of the assistant's chair. The ointment jar held by the assistant is yellow.

16. *The dispensary* [I,23; f.250r]

This view of the dispensary is prompted by the provision of two receipts for depilatory ointments in the treatment of tinea. The collaboration of doctor and assistant is particularly clear, for the latter appears to be relating information to the former (the only comparable example is fig. 43 involving the patient rather than the assistant). The jars on the right are boldly coloured yellow and green. The escutcheons, which remain something of a puzzle, resemble those depicted in fig. 11. The second of the shallow basins has some green colouring. Elsewhere there are faint splashes of yellow.

17. *Treatment of Scrofulous Sores* [I,25; f.251v]

According to the accompanying text mobile scrofulous sores in the head are treated as follows. The doctor takes the head of the scrofula between his fingers and cuts the skin longitudinally, removing the skin with a surgical chisel (*spatumen*, 'cisol'). This is what is depicted in the illustration and not, as M.R. James would have it, 'Doctor hammers a bar into the head of the patient'. For the first time the patient, unassisted, has a chair of his own. In what really forms a doublet with the right-hand illustration of fig. 7 the artist has once again depicted the mallet, which, though not mentioned in the text, is a practical necessity. The patient's posture is striking, as if he is steadying his head against the pressure of the chiselling. The doctor is shown concentrating intently on his work. This is the third time that the artist has combined two stages of an operation in something like a mirror image with its own sense of balance (see figs. 5 & 7). In the right-hand picture the patient is depicted with shaven head, in accordance with the text, and the doctor holds a cloth (soaked in egg-white), and what appears to be a sponge, which, though not mentioned in the text, is a perfectly natural addition by the artist, who understood the need for thorough cleansing of the infected scalp. The patient again has his hand to his head as in the left-hand illustration and a notch in the cranium is clearly visible. On the left the chisel and the head of the mallet are coloured green, as is the left-hand upright of the doctor's chair.

18. *Unspecified Operation* [f.252r]

This illustration resembles part of fig. 5 where the patient kneels
before the doctor who incises the headwound with a sharp
razor-like knife. Here, though, it has no evident relation to the
accompanying text, which, with its directions for the preparation
of a powder, might be expected to have inspired another view of
the dispensary. The picture is incomplete, the patient's chair never
having been drawn in. It is possible that the illustration is displaced
from the verso of the page where it would fittingly illustrate the
making of a cruciform incision in the cranium as part of the
treatment for 'mania et melancholia' (I,26). The blade of the knife
is green, the handle yellow.

19. *Treatment of Scrofulous Sores* [I,25; f.252v]

The illustration accompanies a section dealing with the difficult case where the scrofula is so located that the *dura mater* is infected and the scrofula seems to be growing on the scalp or cranium itself. The area around the infected spot should be pierced with a borer or trephine and scraped clean with a chisel (*spatumen*). The two procedures seem to have been reversed by the artist who shows the chisel (cf. figs. 7 & 17) in use on the left and the borer (cf. figs. 7 & 32) on the right. The mallet takes the form of that depicted in fig. 17. It seems likely that this illustration is an erroneous repetition of fig.17 and that it should really be replaced by fig.18 which has been misplaced on f. 252r, in which case the two illustrations would depict the treatment for 'mania et melancholia' ('deverie' in the Anglo-Norman text) (I,26), in which, incidentally, the patient is to be bound (cf. fig. 35). In the left-hand picture the patient's seat has not been drawn in (cf. figs. 18 & 32). The patient himself looks remarkably at ease. The doctor's posture recalls that of fig. 12. In the right-hand picture the doctor is bearded and the patient's head has been shaved. The patient's hands seem to miss the body of the doctor (were they intended to be bound, as specified in I,26?) and the position of the latter's legs seems unusually awkward for this artist. In the left-hand picture the blade of the chisel and the head of the mallet are coloured green and there are touches of the same colour on the edges of the chair. There is no colour in the right-hand picture. The illustration is another example of mirror image technique (cf. fig. 7).

20. *Treatment for External Worm* [I,55; f.253r]

This section of text is displaced in the MS, for in Roger's *Chirurgia* it forms the penultimate chapter of Book One. When worm has entered the ear it is expelled by instilling into the ear a mixture of oil and the juice of the leaves of honeysuckle and calamint. The doctor is here shown pouring the mixture from a vessel or phial into a funnel (not specified in the text) and thence into the ear (cf. fig. 40). The patient, at ease with arms folded, reclines on a mattress. The posture of both figures suggests a calm, steady operation without movement or agitation, the frontal pose of the doctor resembling that of figs. 17 & 18. The funnel is coloured green and there are splashes of pale yellow on the hatched bed and on the seat.

21. *An Exploratory Operation* [II,1; f.254r]

The displacement of material continues with this section which really forms the first chapter of Book Two of the *Chirurgia*. The illustration is a puzzling exception to the artist's normal practice in that it appears to depart from the accompanying text, which deals with neckwounds where the injury has been caused by a sword or similar weapon. The first step in that case is to look carefully to see if there is any object or matter which must be removed from the wound. A thorough investigation must be made by digital palpation and this is what is depicted in the illustration; only the site of the injury has been transferred to the abdomen, possibly to make the illustration clearer. It is not certain whether the instrument in the doctor's right hand is a probe, a scalpel or (more probably) a needle for stitching the wound. This is the only scene in which the operating table is depicted. The assistant looks on intently, whilst the gaze of the doctor indicates that he is being guided by touch. Note that the doctor never gives up his chair and the artist never neglects the treatment of folds and drapes. The patient appears comfortable. No colour is used in this illustration.

22. *Ligature of Neckwound* [II,3; f.254v]

The displacement of material continues. The accompanying text gives directions for wounds in the neck caused by a sword or similar weapon, specifically where the 'organic' (i.e. jugular) vein has been punctured. The hole in the vein must be promptly sewn up with a needle and thread, whilst on the other side of the injured vessel a ligature must be made. After this the wound is to be dressed with the ordinary dressing of egg-albumen. There is no colour. The illustration closely resembles fig. 41, which is a repetition caused by the displacement of the rest of II,3 to f. 266r–v. As so often the artist has ensured striking parallelism in the leg movements of doctor and patient.

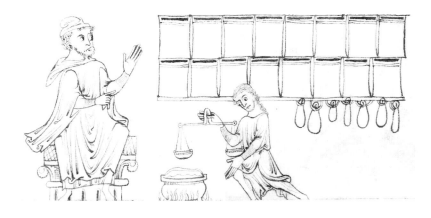

23. *The Dispensary* [I,28; f.255r]

The illustration is prompted by the occurrence in the text of a receipt for the treatment of superfluous eyelashes. The doctor's headgear is new and he gives instructions to an assistant who wears his hair in the manner previously associated with the patient (cf. figs. 17 & 19). This time the assistant himself holds the balances. The storage jars recall those in figs. 3 & 8 and the pouches those shown in figs. 3, 11, & 33. There is no colour.

24. *Leucoma* [I,31; f.255v]

The accompanying text treats the eye complaint leucoma (*panniculum oculorum*). Here the doctor is shown receiving the patient whose leucoma the artist has sought to render by diminishing the size of the pupils. The patient's gesture illustrates his request for advice to which the doctor responds with raised left hand which consistently represents his issuing of instructions, whether to the patient or to an assistant in the dispensary. The patient is shown with a bonnet in a long sequence of illustrations from this point on.

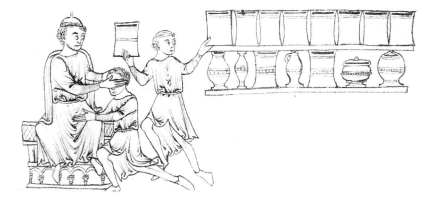

25. *Treatment in the Dispensary* [I,32; f.256r]

The illustration continues to depict the treatment for leucoma. After the scene of diagnosis (fig. 24) we have a view of the dispensary, prompted by the presence in the accompanying text of two lengthy receipts for a corrosive ointment. Here the doctor shields the patient's eyes whilst the assistant selects a jar of ointment in addition to the one he is holding in his right hand. There is no sign of the preparation of medicines and it may be that this is not the dispensary proper but the equivalent of a medicine chest with a good range of made-up medicines (cf. fig. 15). The variously shaped jars recall those of figs. 2 & 8. There is no colour.

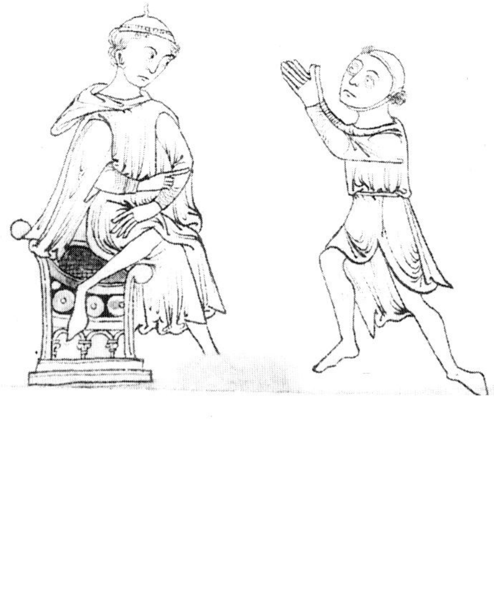

26. *Eye Injury* [I,33–34; f.257v]

The illustration closely resembles fig. 24 since the accompanying text deals once more with leucoma, as well as inflammation and swelling of the eye (in Roger's treatise the chapter heading is *De rubore oculorum et inflacione et panniculo*, 'On inflammation, swelling and web in the eyes'). The patient here appears more agitated, perhaps because his condition is the result of recent injury. His gesture represents a request for help (cf. fig. 34) and the artist has again diminished the size of the pupils in order to convey the notion of eye disease, as well as depicting the patient with raised eyes. The doctor's posture recalls that in fig. 19. There are splashes of green and yellow on the doctor's seat.

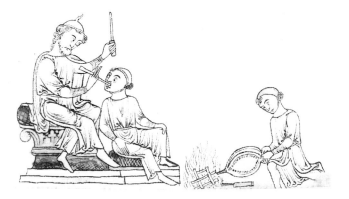

27. *Fistula* [I,36; f.258r]

Here is one of the more painful operations, when a fistula is located
in the region between the eye and nose. The patient is instructed
to avert his eye and the fistula is incised and a feather dipped in
egg-white is inserted in the wound. The roots of the fistula are then
seared by taking an iron or bronze tube ('chalmel de fer u de
araim') (in the doctor's left hand) through which is passed a red
hot iron (in the doctor's right hand) or, if the patient is afraid of
fire, recourse may be had to a corrosive ointment in pill form made
up of quicklime and a lye. The doctor would appear to be
left-handed in this particular picture. The assistant is shown with
bellows and a cautery iron lies heating in the fire. Green and
yellow are used on the doctor's seat and the assistant's bellows and
cap are washed with yellow. Also coloured yellow are the doctor's
beard, the cannula and the handle of the iron.

28. *Examination of Nasal Growth* [I,37; f.258v]

The accompanying text deals with nasal growths and swellings which are not actually polyps. The artist has accordingly depicted the patient with swollen, misshapen nose, undergoing a careful examination by the doctor who, for the first time, without his assistant, touches the patient with both hands. The parallelism of the leg movements is here particularly pronounced and again evokes the cooperation of the two figures in what is a diagnostic examination and not a treatment (the latter involves the use of a chisel or *spatumen* and a short-handled lancet called a *sagittella*). There is no colour.

29. The Dispensary [I,37; f.259r]

The chapter on nasal growths contains a receipt for the preparation of green ointment, thus prompting this depiction of the dispensary. The doctor holds a scroll (often found in Roman sculptures of doctors) which may be compared with the book in fig.6. For the first time *three* assistants are shown at work. The first takes two bundles of herbs from a heavily laden tray of *materia medica* (cf. figs. 3 & 11) – the receipt mentions celandine, wood sorrel, clary, lovage and scabious, specifying a handful of each. The second assistant pounds them with the, here customary, two pestles, and the third assistant holds herbs above a cauldron over a fire. All these stages are referred to in the receipt. There is no colour.

30. *Nasal Polyp* [I,39-40; f.259v]

This illustration follows closely the operation described in the accompanying text. There are two types of polyp, one curable, the other not. When the nose is soft and tractable the polyp is to be cured by taking a pair of small forceps ('deliees tenailles') and extracting it. If the polyp does not come away, the nostril should be enlarged with a tent of earth-nut (*malum terre*) so that an iron or brass tube, hollow like a reed, may be inserted to sear the affected spot. This is obviously what is depicted in the picture. But in fig. 27 the artist included a pair of bellows for heating the cauterizing iron which is placed in the tube. The Latin original makes it clear that this is what happens in the treatment of polyps too (though the bellows are not specifically mentioned). The Anglo-Norman translator, however, through eyeskip (i.e. inadvertently copying from a later occurrence of the same word or phrase) which is characteristic of him, has omitted the detail of the hot iron used for searing. It seems clear, therefore, that the absence of the bellows in this illustration is explained by the fact that the artist followed carefully the Anglo-Norman text before him and not the Latin original. There is no colour.

31. *Treatment of Facial Tumours* [I,44; f.260r]

This illustration is less closely linked to the accompanying text than the others. The left-hand drawing probably represents treatment for a nasal tumour, but it is not clear what object or instrument the doctor is holding in his right hand (a sponge for washing?). On the right he is clearly wielding a razor, which is specifically mentioned in the text. The operation is evidently painful and the assistant stands astride the patient to steady him. The contrary movements of the patient's and assistant's arms and the patient's and doctor's legs show to perfection the artist's concern for a balanced composition. There is no colour.

32. *The Dispensary* [I,44-45; f.260v]

This further view of the dispensary is occasioned by the occurrence of a number of receipts in the accompanying text concerning the treatment of tumours. The patient's face or nose is bandaged and, as in figs. 15 & 25, treatment is taking place in the dispensary itself. As is the case in figs. 18, 19, & 44, the patient's seat has not been drawn in. The assistant is shown bare-headed and with a different hair style from previous representations. The jars (it is interesting that no glass jars are depicted by the present artist) recall those depicted in figs. 2, 8, 25 & 33. There is no colour.

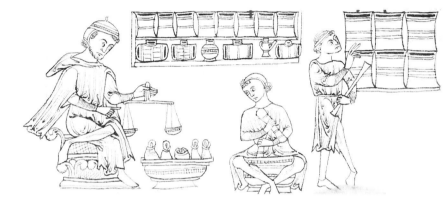

33. *The Dispensary*   [I,45; f.261r]

Another illustration of the dispensary, prompted by the appearance of a receipt 'por manger le cancre' in the Anglo-Norman text. The doctor once more holds the balances, as in figs. 3, 11 & 38 and the pouches recall those shown in figs. 3, 11 & 23. The variously shaped jars are also seen in figs. 2, 8 & 32. The second assistant is holding a stirrer (cf. figs. 8 & 48). There is no colour.

34. *Dislocation of the Jaw?*   [I,47; f.262r]

In the left-hand picture the doctor is seated with a staff (cf. the caduceus of fig. 9) and addresses the patient who approaches with his hands held in a gesture of a request for help (cf. figs. 24 & 26). The patient's swollen right cheek is perhaps to be interpreted, in the light of the text, as an indication of mandibular dislocation in which the upper teeth do not meet with the corresponding members of the lower jaw. The patient's costume is fuller than usual. In the right-hand picture the doctor appears to be wielding a knife, but this can have no relation to the accompanying text – also, the patient's hands appear to be tied. If the swollen cheek in the two pictures is supposed to indicate some sort of growth, they must be displaced from several pages earlier (see fig. 31). Perhaps the artist lost his place or confused the two chapters. In the left-hand picture the doctor's staff and seat are splashed with yellow, as are the folds of his and the patient's garments. In the right-hand picture the blade of the knife and the base of the seat are coloured green, whilst there is yellow on hatched areas, the doctor's and patient's cap and the assistant's headband.

35. *Fistula* [I,51; f.262v]

The illustration refers to a type of fistula or tumour on the jaw which is treated with a tent of earth-nut or a pad of cloth soaked in egg albumen (cf. fig. 32). As in fig. 34 the patient's hands appear to be tied. The bandage appears to be holding a pad in place. Once again (cf. figs. 7 & 10) the doctor's garment displays an elaborate fastening. His chair, the design of which recalls figs. 4, 8, 11, 12, 20, 36, 39, 46, is decorated with yellow and green. The patient's bandage is washed with yellow.

36. *Toothache* [I,52] and *Facial Spots* [I,53; f.263r]

Here the treatment depicted on the left is for toothache in the gums. A cautery (*coctura*, 'quichun') is to be applied to the fontanel. Then seeds of henbane and leek are placed over coals and the patient made to inhale the vapour through a tube or funnel (*canellum emboti*, 'chalmel qui est apelé embottun'). The artist has failed to depict this tube and again the explanation seems to reside in a pecularity of the Anglo-Norman translation. For 'chalmel' the scribe has written 'chaval' (possibly for 'chanal' = *canellum*) which would be incomprehensible to the artist, who was no more likely to have known what the *embottum* of the Latin original looked like either. The seat and the cauldron are decorated in yellow and green. The right-hand picture presents a rather obvious case of facial spots ('borbelettes'). As before (see figs. 24 & 26), the patient's clasped hands indicate his request for help and the doctor's raised index finger represents the authoritative imparting of information (cf. figs. 2, 6, 9, 15, 26). Once again (see figs. 5, 7 & 31) in a 'double scene' the artist has adopted the mirror image technique. There are touches of green and yellow on the doctor's seat, and the folds of his garment are touched with green.

37. Morphew [I,53; f.264r]

The illustration depicts the diagnosis of *morphea alba*, a type of leprosy which was curable (*morphea nigra* was not). To establish which type the patient was suffering from his skin was punctured with a needle (here held by the doctor in his right hand): if blood issued, he was curable; if a white liquid oozed forth, he was not. In the illustration both seats are decorated with green, as are the folds of the doctor's garment and the cord around his cap.

38. *The Dispensary* [I,53; f.265r]

This view of the dispensary, the fullest of all, is prompted by a receipt for an ointment for treating *morphea nigra*. As well as standard storage jars and the characteristically varied vessels and pouches, there is a striking display of vegetable products on the top row of shelves. The tray of *materia medica* shows the artist's habitual attention to detail and formal variety (cf. figs. 3, 11 & 29). The doctor, again holding balances (cf. figs. 3, 11 & 33) is depicted with a lap dog (coloured yellow). The herbs, both hanging and laid out, are coloured green, the jars are yellow. Green has also been applied to the cauldron and basin, whilst the pestles and fireplace are touched with yellow.

39. *Ear-ache* [I,54; f.265v]

This illustration, exceptionally, seems to have nothing at all to do with the accompanying text besides the fact that the medical problem being treated is ear-ache. The doctor is strangely reduced in size, his legs of startling thinness. The patient's hands are clasped in a relaxed gesture, but it is not clear what operation the doctor is performing on his ear. Parts of the seat, the folds of garments and the blade of the knife are washed in green.

40. *Ear-ache* [I,54; f.266r]

According to the accompanying text (begun on the previous page) wormwood, calamint, savin and oil from the henbane seed are to be placed in a suitable vessel against the open end of which is to be held a funnel (*embotum*, cf. fig. 20), so that the vapour enters the patient's ear. The figure of the patient appears truncated and the sweep of the leg movements isolates the unnatural position and proportion of the patient's arms, a rare failing in this artist. The doctor wears ermine (cf. fig. 4). The funnel is coloured green and there are pale splashes of yellow on folds of the garments and on the hatching of the doctor's seat.

41. *Ligature of Neckwound* [II,2; f.266v]

Here the doctor stitches a wound in the patient's neck in an illustration which is really a repetition of fig. 22 prompted by the displacement in the Anglo-Norman translation where I,55–II,3 are suddenly interposed on folios 253r–255r and II,3 then continued on folio 266r–v. The consequent splitting of II,3 has led the artist faithfully to illustrate it twice. Comparison of the two illustrations reveal many differences of detail within a consistently conceived overall composition. In fig. 22 the patient's head is more aptly cradled in the doctor's right arm and at a more appropriate level for intricate suturing, but in fig. 41 the less dynamic position of the doctor's and patient's legs gives a more suitable impression of calm immobility. There are traces of yellow splashing on folds of the garments and on the base and hatched area of the doctor's seat.

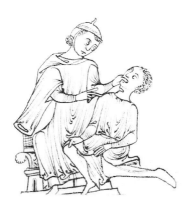

42. *Throatwound* [II,6; f.267r]

Here the doctor inspects the patient's throat, with its clearly visible
wound, in order to diagnose the nature of the injury, for if the
oesophagus or tracheal artery are punctured or severed, the
outcome is fatal. M.R. James identified the picture with the
caption 'He [sc. the doctor] presses his thumb into the mouth of
the patient'. In fact, the doctor is pushing the patient's head back
in order to get a clearer look at his throat. This is one of the few
illustrations where the artist has sought to render any form of
physical force, though the patient remains composed, his hands in
a relaxed pose. There are a few splashes of yellow.

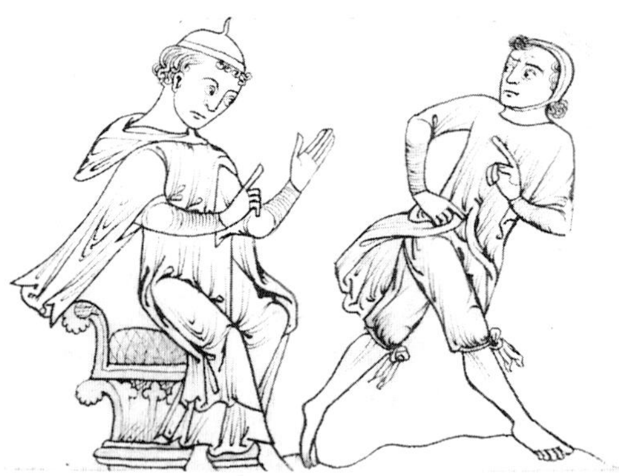

43. *Swelling in the Kidneys* [II,9; f.268r]

In this illustration the patient adopts an unusually active role as is made clear from the gestures depicted. The manual gesture of the doctor shows that he is the recipient of information being supplied by the patient (cf. fig. 16), whose left hand is raised in the conventional signal of instruction. With his right hand he is probably indicating his kidneys (an addition of the Anglo-Norman translator) where there is a carbuncular swelling described in the Anglo-Norman as *anthrax* or *carbunculus*. His contorted body movement is meant to indicate pain. This is one of the few illustrations in which the patient is shown actively explaining his symptoms whilst the doctor listens. The patient is shown in shirt and breeches (cf. figs. 14 & 48), enabling him to indicate more precisely the area of pain. His rather apprehensive expression led M.R. James to describe him as 'an excited man in shirt and drawers points to his stomach' and Sudhoff to believe that he was escaping in fright after hearing of the need for surgery! The doctor is calm and reassuring. There are a few splashes of yellow.

44. *The Dispensary* [II,12; f.269r]

This view of the dispensary, with the reappearance of surgical instruments (cf. fig. 2), is occasioned by a receipt in the text for an ointment for treatment of tumour in the neck. The doctor gives instructions to the assistant, whose seat has not been drawn in by the artist (cf. figs. 18, 19, & 32). Hanging from the wall are a claw-bar, a trephine (?), and a hook (*uncus*, 'fer rebuchié' – see II,13), though the accompanying text formally excludes surgical intervention! (cf. no. 47 below). There is green colouring on the doctor's seat, the second surgical instrument, and the assistant's pestles and mortar.

45. *Scrofulous Sores in the Throat* [II,13; f.269v]

The illustration concerns scrofulous growths in the throat. The doctor inspects the patient's throat for signs of scrofula or glanders. There is less detail than usual and the hang of the doctor's cloak over his right shoulder is unnatural, but the patient's nervous response is well conveyed. There is no colour.

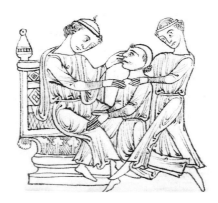

46. *Inspection of the Throat* [II,13; f.270v]

The illustration appears to represent an external inspection of the throat (cf. fig. 42) for signs of swelling, the doctor holding up the patient's head to obtain a better view of the throat. The collaboration of the assistant seems unnecessary. The picture is only loosely related to the accompanying text which deals with surgical intervention for swellings in the throat. Perhaps the artist intended to equip the doctor with a knife in his right hand and forgot to execute it.

47. *Throat Inspection* [? ; f.271r]

There is no clear connection between this illustration and the accompanying text. It is surprising that the patient's mouth is closed. The doctor is perhaps once more holding up the patient's head to gain better access to the throat, though this is not clearly the case here. M.R. James thought that the doctor 'applies a tool to the lower jaw of the patient held by a woman (?)'. It is not obvious what the instrument held by the doctor is. (The cautery is specifically ruled out by the text.) The assistant is certainly not a woman. His headress may be compared with that worn by Tristan in a set of drawings in MS British Library, Add. 11619 (esp. ff. 6r, 7v, & 8r). There is no colour.

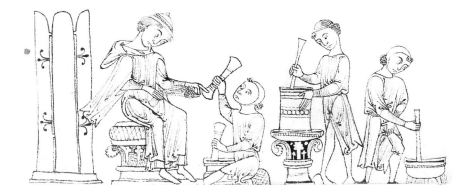

48. The Dispensary [II,14; f.272r]

This last view of the dispensary is prompted by a receipt for an ointment to treat fistula. There now appears a third assistant (cf. fig. 29) stirring ingredients in a jar placed on a shallow dish on top of a stand shaped like the capital of a column. On the left are doors. The doctor directs the first assistant, whilst holding a bunch of herbs in his right hand. There is no colour.

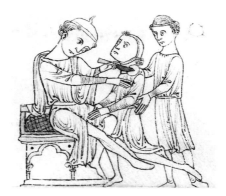

49. *Fistula (?)* [f.273r]

This illustration appears to deal with the lancing of a fistula. There is no definitive link with the accompanying text which describes the treatment of bronchocele or goitre which may involve cutting. The preceding section (II,14) deals with fistula on the neck but formally excludes cutting. The patient exhibits an obvious growth at the base of his neck and this is being incised with a *rasorium*. The handle of the knife is yellow, the blade green.

50. *Doctor* [f.273v]

This uncompleted illustration is not by the principal artist. The doctor is normally depicted with a more rounded face and different shaped nose, and never in profile like this. The caption reads 'Pater est alpha et o[mega], filius est vita, spiritus sanctus est remedium' (see Introduction p. xvi).

Bibliography

Listed below are works in which some (but never all) of the medical drawings from MS Trinity College, Cambridge, O.1.20 have been reproduced.

Cianciòlo, U., 'Il compendio provenzale verseggiato della Chirurgia di Ruggero da Salerno', *Archivum Romanicum* 25 (1941) [1–85] tav.IV [5 drawings]

De Moulin, D., *A History of Surgery with emphasis on the Netherlands* (Dordrecht etc., 1988), p.39 [3 drawings]

Dressendörfer, W., 'Französische Apothekendarstellungen aus dem 13. Jahrhundert', *Beiträge zur Geschichte der Pharmazie* 31, viii (1980), 57–61 [6 drawings of the dispensary]

Herrlinger, R., *Geschichte der medizinischen Abbildung I Von der Antike bis um 1600* (München, 1967), p.44 & fig.43 [1 drawing]

Huard, P. & Grmek, M.D., *Mille Ans de chirurgie en Occident: Ve – XVe siècles* (Paris, 1966), pp.60–95 [36 drawings], 167–8 [captions]

MacKinney, L., *Medical Illustrations in Medieval Manuscripts* (London, 1965) p.71 & fig.71 [1 drawing]

Morgan, Nigel, *A Survey of Manuscripts Illuminated in the British Isles* vol.4 *Early Gothic Manuscripts [1] 1190–1250* (Oxford, 1982), pp.126–7, illustr. nos. 256–61 [6 drawings]

Paterson, Linda, 'Military Surgery: Knights, Sergeants and Raimon of Avignon's Version of the *Chirurgia* of Roger of Salerno (1180–1209)', in C. Harper-Bill & R. Harvey (eds.), *The Ideals and Practice of Medieval Knighthood: Papers from the third Strawberry Hill Conference 1986* (Woodbridge, 1988) [pp.117–46] figs.9–18 [10 drawings]

Sudhoff, K., *Beiträge zur Geschichte der Chirurgie im Mittelalter*, Teil 1 Studien zur Geschichte der Medizin 10 (Leipzig, 1914), pp.33–42, plates V–VII [45 drawings]

Tabanelli, M., *Techniche e strumenti chirurgici del XIII e XIV secolo* (Firenze, 1973), pp.68–71 & fig.4b.

For a description of MS Cambridge, Trinity College O.1.20 see Tony Hunt, *Popular Medicine in Thirteenth-century England* (Cambridge, 1990), pp.142–44. M.R. James's description of the drawings appears in his *The Western Manuscripts in the Library of Trinity College, Cambridge: a descriptive catalogue* 3 (Cambridge, 1902), pp.23–8.

The only study of Roger Frugard is A. Pazzini, *Ruggero di Giovanni Frugardo maestro di chirurgia a Parma e l'opera sua* (Roma, 1966)

The most useful introduction to early surgical writing is D. De Moulin, *A History of Surgery with emphasis on the Netherlands* (Dordrecht, 1988)

On medical illustrations see Peter Murray Jones, *Medieval Medical Miniatures* (London, 1984)